Extreme Sports

Weight Lifting

by Bill Lund

C A P S T O N E   P R E S S

M A N K A T O ,   M I N N E S O T A

C A P S T O N E   P R E S S
818 North Willow Street • Mankato, MN 56001

Printed in the United States of America.

Library of Congress Cataloging-in-Publication Data
Lund, Bill, 1954-
  Weight lifting/by Bill Lund.
    p. cm. -- (Extreme sports)
  Includes bibliographical references and index.
  Summary: Describes the history, equipment, and contemporary practice
of weight lifting.
  ISBN 1-56065-431-7
  1. Weight lifting-Juvenile literature. [1. Weight lifting.] I. Title. II. Series.
GV546.3.L86 1996
796.41--dc20

                                        96-24725
                                        CIP
                                        AC

Photo credits
Vic Boff, 25. International Stock/Carolin Wood, 12.
Unicorn/Chris Boylan, 40; Rod Furgason, 38; Kathy Hamer,
14; Karen Holsinger, 8; Martha McBride, 10, 26, 30, 32, 36;
John W. Mayo, 22; Mike Morris, 20; Alon Reininger, 17;
Mary Stadtfeld, 34; Larry Stanley, 6; Dick Young, cover, 4,
19, 28. U.S. Weightlifting Federation, 42.

Table of Contents

Chapter 1 Muscles.................................... 5

Chapter 2 Building Muscle 11

Chapter 3 Kinds of Weight Lifting................. 15

Chapter 4 Working With Weights 27

Chapter 5 The Lifting Lifestyle 33

Chapter 6 Safe Lifting.................................. 39

Photo Diagram.................................... 36

Glossary 44

To Learn More 45

Useful Addresses 46

Internet Sites..................................... 47

Index 48

Words in **boldface** type in the text are defined
in the Glossary in the back of this book.

Chapter 1

Muscles

Weight lifting is a popular sport. Different weight lifters want different things. But their basic goal is the same. They use weights to develop their muscles. In the world of weight lifting, muscles are everything.

Your muscles work every minute of every day. You use muscles when you run or walk. You use muscles when you throw a ball or lift it from the ground.

Even when you are not thinking about it, you are using muscles. Every time you blink your eyes, you are using muscles. Every time

Weight lifters share a common goal. They all want to develop their muscles.

you smile, you are using muscles. You use muscles every time you breathe.

Your heart is a muscle. As long as you are alive, your heart never stops working. Muscles are the engines that keep your body running.

Small and Large Muscles

The human body has about 800 different muscles. Some of them are very small. Small muscles make small movements. Small muscles raise your big toe. Small muscles move your eyes so you can look to the left or to the right.

Some muscles are very large. The muscles in your thighs, arms, shoulders, and back are large muscles. Large muscles can do great feats of strength.

Weight Lifting

Some people lift weights to make themselves stronger for other sports. Many

The large muscles in the arms can do great feats of strength.

Many people lift weights to feel better about themselves.

football players lift weights. So do wrestlers, baseball players, and basketball players.

Some people use weight lifting to make their bodies look better. They want to look bigger. They want to look more muscular.

Other people lift weights to build strength. They work so they can lift heavier and heavier weights. Many of these weight lifters enter competitions.

History

People have lifted stones and weights to test their strength for thousands of years. Many of the early weight lifters were good at putting on spectacular shows. They dressed in wild costumes and gave themselves such names as Saxon and Sandow. They were a lot like today's professional wrestlers.

Sandow was from Germany. His real name was Karl Frederick Mueller. It is said that he could lift a 600-pound (270-kilogram) weight with his middle finger.

Sandow used to cover his body in white powder. Then he performed his lifting feats in front of a black curtain. This made him look like a living statue.

Weight lifting became a medal sport at the 1896 Olympic Games in Athens, Greece. Standard rules were created. By the early 1900s, weight lifting had become popular, especially in Europe.

Chapter 2
Building Muscle

W eight lifters use barbells, dumbbells, and weight machines to work their muscles. This makes them stronger and larger.

When weight lifters lift weights, their muscles flex. When muscles flex they need extra oxygen. A weight lifter's body sends the extra oxygen to the muscles though the blood.

To make sure the oxygen gets to the blood, the body opens blood vessels in the muscles. The weight lifter's heart beats faster. The muscles get bigger and stronger when more blood is pumped into them.

Weight lifters use dumbbells to make their muscles bigger and stronger.

Getting a Pump

When weight lifters work their muscles hard, the muscles immediately get bigger. They stay bigger for a while. They get hard. They might even tingle.

Weight lifters call this feeling a pump. A weight lifter's skin can turn a rosy color over a pumped muscle. The rosy color is from the extra blood that the heart has pumped there.

Weight lifters lose this pump a short time after they stop lifting. If they keep lifting regularly, though, their muscles will get bigger and stay that way. When the muscles get bigger, they get stronger, too.

Muscles get bigger and harder after a workout. This is called a pump.

Chapter 3

Kinds of Weight Lifting

P eople lift weights for different reasons. Some weight lifters want to get strong. Some want to increase the size of their muscles. People lift weights in different ways to reach their different goals.

Strength Training

Many athletes lift weights to make them better at other sports. They might be swimmers or hockey players or soccer players. No matter what their sport is, they can do better if they are stronger.

Many young athletes lift weights to make themselves better at other sports.

Football linebackers need power to break through the line and make tackles. Quarterbacks need a strong throwing arm and powerful legs for running. Swimmers need strong arms for stroking and strong legs for kicking. Basketball players need jumping and passing power.

Most lifters working on strength training are not concerned about making their muscles bigger. They want their muscles to be strong and flexible.

A swimmer, for example, wants muscles that are strong, but not too large. Large muscles add resistance in the water. Resistance slows a swimmer.

Bodybuilding

Bodybuilders are men and women who want to make their bodies look lean and muscular. Many bodybuilders enter judged competitions. The judges pick the best-built bodybuilder in

Bodybuilders want to look lean and muscular.

different categories. The categories are divided by body weight.

Bodybuilders lift weights to increase the size of their muscles. Size, though, is not everything in bodybuilding. Bodybuilders must also be lean. When bodybuilders are lean, they look cut. Cut means their muscles are sharp and well defined.

To get lean, bodybuilders lower the fat in their bodies. They go on special low-fat diets. They do fat-burning **aerobic** exercises.

The body of an average healthy athlete has between 12 percent and 20 percent body fat. Bodybuilders preparing for competition cannot have that much body fat. They try to lower their body fat to around 6 percent.

Arnold Schwarzenegger

Arnold Schwarzenegger was a famous bodybuilder. He later became a world-famous actor. His movies have been some of the most popular ones of all time.

Bodybuilders look cut.

Schwarzenegger is from Austria. He has won many bodybuilding contests. In 1966, he won the Mr. Europe and Best-Built Man of Europe contests. He became Mr. Universe in 1967.

Schwarzenegger moved to the United States in 1968. He won the Mr. Universe title five more times and the Mr. Olympia title seven times before retiring. He starred in a surprisingly successful bodybuilding documentary called *Pumping Iron*.

Schwarzenegger then became a star in many popular action-adventure movies. He also starred in the comedies *Kindergarten Cop* and *Twins*. In 1990, Schwarzenegger served as the chair of the President's Council on Physical Fitness and Sports.

Competitive Weight Lifting and Power Lifting

Competitive weight lifters and power lifters are usually the strongest of all lifters. These men and women compete against other lifters who weigh about as much as they do. Their

Power lifters are some of the strongest weight lifters.

WEIGHT ON BAR
121 ¼ LBS.

Competitive weight lifters must bring the weight over their heads.

goal is to lift the greatest amount of weight. Competitive weight lifters compete in two events. One event is the clean and jerk. The clean and jerk is a lift in which the barbell is lifted from the floor to the chest, and then thrust directly overhead so that the arms are completely extended.

Another event is the snatch. The snatch is a lift in which the barbell is raised in one continuous motion from the floor directly over the lifter's head, with the arms completely extended. Unlike the clean and jerk, the lifter does not pause with the barbell at his or her chest

In both events, the lifters must bring the weight fully off the ground. They must raise it above their heads. When the lifters have the weight under control, they can drop it to the floor.

Power Lifting

Power lifters compete in three events. One event is the squat. For the squat, lifters start with the bar on their shoulders. They lower themselves into a squatting position and then stand up again.

Another event is the bench press. For the bench press, lifters lie on a padded bench. They raise and lower a barbell from their chest to arm's length.

The third event is the dead lift. For the dead lift, lifters reach down and grab a barbell from the floor. They stand up, lifting the weight with their legs and back. The bar hangs at arm's length.

Record Holders

Weight lifting competitions are held in more than 100 countries around the world. Weight lifting is now organized and governed by the International Weightlifting Federation. Both men and women compete. These weight lifters and power lifters have set amazing records.

One of the famous early weight lifters was Canada's Louis Cyr. He competed in the late 1800s. He stood 5 feet 10 inches (178 centimeters) tall. He weighed 300 pounds (135 kilograms).

Cyr's enormous **biceps** measured 20 inches (51 centimeters) around. His thighs measured 33 inches (84 centimeters). His most famous feat of strength was lifting 4,300 pounds (1,935 kilograms) in a dead lift.

John Henry Davis was an undefeated weight lifting champion from 1938 to 1953. He was from the United States. He was the first amateur weight lifter to clean and jerk 400 pounds (180 kilograms).

Louis Cyr, from Canada, had biceps that measured 20 inches (51 centimeters) around.

Lorraine Constanzo holds the women's power lifting record. She is from the United States. In 1987, she squatted 628 pounds (283 kilograms).

Chapter 4
Working With Weights

W eight lifting is one of the best ways to gain strength and muscle size. Free weights can be used with dumbbells and barbells. Weight lifters can use lifting machines, too.

Lifting Machines

Many gyms have weight-lifting machines. These machines have different stations. Lifters can work on different muscle groups at each station.

Weights are stacked at each station. A pin is used to adjust the weight. Each lifter can change the weight to match his or her strength.

Weight lifting machines can be found at many gyms.

Many lifters say that machines do not work their muscles as well as free weights.

Weight machines are expensive. They take up a lot of space. They are usually found in gyms, rather than in lifters' homes. Many lifters say that machines do not work their muscles as well as free weights.

Barbells and Dumbbells

Beginning weight lifters often buy their own set of equipment. This lets them work out at home. Beginning equipment should include at least 100 pounds (45 kilograms) of free weights. It should also include a padded bench.

The equipment should include a long bar. Weights are attached to the ends of the bar. This makes a barbell.

The equipment should also include a pair of shorter bars. Weights can be attached to these, too. This makes dumbbells.

Weight lifters often progress quickly during their first year in the sport. Many of them get more serious about weight lifting. They usually want to increase the amount of weight they work out with. That way they will continue to get stronger.

The most serious weight lifters probably want to start going to a gymnasium. Most gymnasiums offer better lifting equipment. They have heavier weights, stronger bars, and weight machines.

The Bench Press and The Curl

There are many exercises lifters can do with weights. One exercise is called the bench press. Weight lifters lie on their backs to do the bench

Weight lifters hold the barbell on their shoulders to do squats.

press. They push a barbell or a pair of dumbbells up from their chest. This exercise works mainly the **pectoral muscles**.

Another exercise is called a curl. Weight lifters stand to do a curl. They hold a barbell or dumbbell at arm's length. They curl toward their body. This works mainly their biceps.

The Fly and The Squat

Another exercise is called a fly. It works muscles in the arms, shoulders, and chest.

Weight lifters lie on their backs to do a fly. They hold a pair of dumbbells at arm's length above their chest.

When lifters do this exercise, it looks like they are flapping their arms to fly. They hold their arms as straight as possible. Then they bring the weights down to their sides, bending their elbows. Then they lift the dumbbells back up to the starting point.

Another exercise is called a squat. Squats work muscles in the legs. Weight lifters hold the barbell on their shoulders to do squats. Then they squat down until their thighs are almost parallel with the floor. Then they straighten back up again.

Reps and Sets

Weight lifters do reps and sets. Reps stands for repetitions. Reps are the number of times a weight lifter repeats an exercise without stopping.

Sets are the number of batches of reps a lifter does during a workout. A weight lifter might do three sets of curls. Each set might include eight reps.

Chapter 5

The Lifting Lifestyle

Different weight lifters have different goals. Many things besides lifting contribute to a weight lifter's success. Most competitive weight lifters and bodybuilders follow a special lifting lifestyle.

Aerobic Exercise

Many lifters do aerobic exercises. Running and bicycling are popular aerobic exercises. Aerobic exercises increase weight lifters' heart rates. This makes them breathe harder. When they breathe harder, they take in more oxygen.

Many weight lifters do such aerobic exercises as stationary bicycling.

Weight lifters eat foods high in protein to help make their muscles bigger.

When lifters take in more oxygen, they strengthen their hearts and lungs. This keeps them healthier. It also helps keep a lifter's weight down.

Aerobic exercises help lifters lose fat. This is important for bodybuilders. Bodybuilders want to stay as lean as possible.

Nutrition

Smart weight lifters eat the right kinds of food. Weight lifters who eat the best usually have the most success in competitions. The kind of food weight lifters eat depends on their individual goals.

Weight lifters eat **carbohydrates** to get energy. The human body can easily burn carbohydrate calories. These calories are turned into energy. Carbohydrates come from such foods as corn, wheat, rice, potatoes, and fruits.

Weight lifters eat **proteins** to build up their muscles. The body uses protein to build new muscle. Some of the best sources of protein are meat, chicken, fish, eggs, and such dairy products as milk, cheese, and yogurt.

Most weight lifters try to avoid too much fat. Fat is an essential part of our diet. Most people eat more fat than they need, though.

Most lifters also try to avoid too much sugar. They do not eat candy bars or doughnuts. These foods do not provide useful energy.

Sugars do not help build muscles. They only spoil lifters' appetites so they cannot eat the nutritious foods they really need.

Dumbbell

Biceps

Bench

25

Pectorals

Triceps

Foream

Chapter 6
Safe Lifting

W eight lifters use heavy weights. It is easy for lifters to injure themselves. They can even injure others around them. Even a small injury can keep a weight lifter out of the gym for weeks or months.

Stretching

The human body needs to warm up before intense exercise. The muscles need to be stretched. Athletes should break a sweat before they start serious exercise.

Weight lifters should stretch and warm up before they start lifting. This is one of the best

Weight lifters should stretch before they start lifting.

ways to avoid muscle injuries. By taking 10 minutes to stretch before they begin, weight lifters can avoid many serious injuries.

Spotting

For some exercises, weight lifters need someone to watch over them. This person is called a spotter. The spotter takes control of the weight if the lifter cannot handle it anymore.

A spotter is not necessary with some exercises, such as curls. A spotter is very important in other exercises, though, such as the bench press.

A bench-press spotter stands near the lifter's head. The spotter lifts the barbell off the lifter's chest if the weight gets too heavy.

The weights get heavier as lifters advance in the sport. When a lifter uses heavier weights, it is easier to get injured. For that reason, spotters become even more important as weight lifters advance.

Spotters take control of the weight if a lifter needs help.

Competitive weight lifters are tested to make sure they are not using steroids.

Anabolic Steroids

Anabolic steroids are artificial **hormones** that make muscles grow faster and bigger than normal. They are used to treat some diseases. But steroids can be dangerous. They can have many bad side effects. They can kill you.

Unless prescribed by a doctor, steroids are illegal. Still, some weight lifters have used them to get an advantage over their opponents.

Steroid use has given the sport of weight lifting a bad reputation.

Competitive weight lifters are tested to make sure they are not using steroids. In the 1988 Olympics, two Bulgarian lifters tested positive for steroid use. The rest of the Bulgarian weight-lifting team went home without being tested.

Olympic officials have thought about dropping the sport from the Olympics until the steroid problem can be cleared up. They have not taken any action so far, though. Weight lifters who want a long, normal life never take the illegal steroids.

The Desire for Power

Weight lifting makes people stronger. It changes the way they look. Weight lifting makes people feel powerful.

Weight lifting is popular around the world. It gets more popular every year. Some people lift weights to compete. Others do it just to feel better about themselves. Either way, weight lifting is a great way for people to make the most of their muscles.

Glossary

aerobic—exercise that conditions the heart and lungs by making the body use oxygen more efficiently

biceps—the large muscle at the front of the upper arm

carbohydrates—chemical compounds found in such foods as bread, pasta, and potatoes

efficient—to do something with the least amount of effort, expense, or waste

hormones—a substance that travels through bodily fluids from one organ to another organ to produce a specific effect

pectoral muscles—the large muscles at the front of the chest

protein—a chemical compound found in such foods as meat, cheese and peanut butter

To Learn More

Fodor, R.V. and G.J. Taylor. *Junior Body Building: Growing Strong.* New York: Sterling Publishing, 1982.

Sprague, Ken. *Sports Strength.* New York: The Putnam Publishing Group, 1993.

Weider, Joe. *Ultimate Bodybuilding.* New York: Contemporary Books, 1989.

Whitehead, Dr. Nick. *Learn Weight Training in a Weekend.* New York: Alfred A. Knopf, 1992.

Useful Addresses

American Federation of Women Bodybuilders
P.O. Box 363
Niwot, CO 80544-0363

Canadian Weightlifting Federation
333 River Road
Ottawa, ON K1L 8H9
Canada

U.S. Weightlifting Federation
1 Olympic Plaza
Colorado Springs, CO 80909

U.S. Powerlifting Federation
P.O. Box 2170
Kilgore, TX 75663

U.S. Weightlifting Hall of Fame
P.O. Box 1707
York, PA 17405

Internet Sites

Olympic-Style Weightlifting
http://www.waf.com/weights/index.html

Sports on the Net
http://www.shadeslanding.com/sports

The Weight Training Page
http://www.cs.unc.edu/~wilsonk/weights.html

Weightlifting 101
http://www.branch.com/zand/zand.htm

Index

anabolic steroids, 42
Athens, Greece, 9
Austria, 21

bench press, 23, 29, 41
Best-Built Man of Europe, 21
Bulgaria, 43

Canada, 24, 26
carbohydrates, 35, 44
clean and jerk, 22, 24
Constanzo, Lorraine, 25
curl, 29, 30, 31, 41
Cyr, Louis, 24

Davis, John Henry, 24

Europe, 9, 21

fly, 30, 31

Germany, 9

hormones, 42, 44

International Weightlifting
   Federation, 24

Kindergarten Cop, 21

Mr. Olympia, 21
Mr. Universe, 21
Mueller, Karl Frederick, 9

Olympic Games, 9

President's Council on
   Physical Fitness, 21
protein, 35, 44
Pumping Iron, 21

Sandow, 9
Saxon, 9
Schwarzenegger, Arnold, 18,
   21
snatch, 22
squat, 23, 25, 30, 31

Twins, 21

United States, 21, 24, 25

weight machine, 11, 28, 29